A LADY IN A YELLOW DRESS

An inspired woman inspires all.

She embodies sunshine and happiness.

Poems by

Tendai M. Shaba

A LADY IN A YELLOW DRESS

(An inspired woman)

Copyright © 2023 by Tendai M. Shaba

Pachulu Publishing

Republic of Malawi

From the author of Moments to Cherish (2020)

For more information:

http://www.tendaishaba.com/

ISBN: 978-99960-93-54-8

The colour yellow is often associated with sunshine and happiness. These poems are written to inspire good emotional health for all who seek sunshine and happiness within themselves. As much as we are inspired by the good and beautiful things around us, our focal point of inspiration is the lady in a yellow dress.

Table of Contents

A lady in a yellow dress

I see you
A lady in a yellow dress
I see the glow on your face
That colour brings out the happiness in you
It brings out the confidence in you
As you move with optimism
That yellow dress complements
Your laughter
And your friendliness
I see you
Lady in a yellow dress
You look beautiful

SUNSHINE ☼

A ray of sunshine

Bright, you are
A ray of sunshine
Filled with optimism and hope
Filled with faith and courage
You shine not because they tell you to
You shine because you simply have to
It is in your nature to shine your light
To be the brightest light you can be
You are a ray of sunshine

Yellow and gold

Find the courage to smile
You have a beautiful smile
Find the courage to talk
You have a beautiful voice
Find the courage to laugh
You have a beautiful laugh
Find the courage to dream
Your imagination is beautiful
Find the courage to speak your mind
You have beautiful thoughts
You embody the glory of God
You are the embodiment of yellow and gold

Different

You are different
The way you do things
Fueled by your creative spirit
You are different
The way you talk
Empowered by your intellect
You are so different

Moments of gratitude

She's grateful
As she reflects on life every day
Her daily moments of gratitude
She has a big heart, she knows it
She has caring hands, she knows it
She has big plans and she knows it
She serves a big God, she knows it
As she reflects on life every day
Her daily moments of gratitude

Continuous

She knows well enough
But that's never enough
She continues to learn
Such is her level of intellect
She strives to do better
And to be better
Such is her thirst for continuous learning

Spirituality

Words of wisdom feed her spirituality
She is a spiritual woman
Words of prayer are never far from her lips
Inspiration feeds her soulfulness
She is a soulful woman
She feels everything
She sees everything
And she touches everything
Her thoughts and feelings are well aligned
She is a spiritual and soulful woman

See the sunshine

She sees the sunshine and says
'Glory to God, let it shine!'
She takes on the day
With faith in her heart
She is a courageous woman
She braves the dark times, time and time again
And when she sees the sunshine, she says
'Glory to God, let it shine again and again!'

Yellow cup

Her cup of happiness
Her cup of spirituality
Her cup of soulfulness
Her cup of confidence
Her cup of intellect and mindfulness
Her cup of beauty
Her cup of gratitude
Her cup of kindness and humility
She drinks from her yellow cup

The power of yellow

It summons her to greatness
It pushes her to do greater things
It carries her to newer heights
It moves her to greener pastures
It brings out her ambition
And her purpose and meaning
To be the best she can be
To effortlessly run her race
And she does it all with a smile on her face

The colour of healing

She focuses on healing
Her past is her past
As she hopes for better and brighter days
Today is another day
To smile again
To laugh again
And to move again
She focuses on healing
Her past is her past
As she hopes for better and brighter days

Well-being

She is an inspired woman
Her well-being is important
She is an ambitious woman
Her well-being is important
She is a gracious woman
Her well-being is important

A sight to see

So majestically clad in her yellow dress
A sight to see
Happiness personified, in that yellow dress
The brightest ray of sunshine
So vibrant in her yellow dress
A sight to see

Vibrant

Such vibrancy
When I see you in yellow
Such beauty
When I see you in yellow
Such joy and happiness
When I see you in yellow
You are vibrant
Lady in a yellow dress

She wears her confidence

You can see when she walks
So confidently
She displays confidence in her walk
You can see when she talks
So confidently
She displays her confidence in her talk

Glow

She glows differently

Because she is different

She knows her worth

Knows what makes her special

Knows what makes her unique

When she smiles, hard to fake it

When she laughs, hard to fake it

When she feels, hard to fake it
Her smile is real

Her laughter is real

And her feelings are real
That's why she glows differently

She takes her time

Never in a rush
She takes her time
She is confident in the way she does things
So patiently, her moves are well calculated
She is a woman with a plan
She takes her time

Small ideas

She believes in her small ideas
They solve big problems
Her small ideas often become big ideas
She believes in her small ideas

Small plans

She believes in her small plans
They become part of her big picture
Her small plans often become big plans
She believes in her small plans

Small steps

She believes in her small steps
They are part of her journey
Her small steps often become big steps
She believes in her small steps

Small spaces, big spaces

She can handle small spaces
She can handle big spaces
Whichever space she is in
She will make that space her own

Big ideas

Her ideas are big
Because she believes in a big God

25

Big plans

Her plans are big
Because she believes in a big God

Big plans

Her plans are big
Because she believes in a big God

Big steps

Her steps are big
Because she believes in a big God

When she speaks

When she speaks
She speaks truthfully, for herself
And for those who cannot speak for themselves

Character is everything

She is prayerful
She is helpful
She is forgiving
And she is giving
Character is everything

She is worth more

She is worth more than you can imagine
She possesses the character of an excellent lady
The attitude of a hard-working lady
The caring heart of a loving lady
She is worth more than you can imagine

Eloquence

When she speaks, you listen to her eloquence
When she walks, so eloquently
She is charming and amazing
She fears God, worthy to be admired
She epitomizes beauty and excellence
Such is her eloquence

Her God-given freedom

To be all she can be
To do all she can do
She is blessed with strength and dignity
The work of her hands is worthy of rewards
That is her God-given freedom

Wealth, worth and health

She strives to find balance in her life
To accumulate wealth and be wealthy
To have self-belief and be worthy
And to take care of her health and be healthy
She believes in wealth, worth and health

Learning is everything

She lives and learns
Learning to be happy
Learning to love
Learning to trust
Learning to forgive
She lives and learns
Learning is everything
She knows what to do
And how to do it
When God gives her strength
She has the will to do it

Her abundance of grace

She prays to God for abundance
To have blessings in abundance
To have happiness in abundance
To have peace in abundance
She prays to God for abundance
Her abundance of grace

Resourceful

She is resourceful
Not only does she have the knowledge
Have the skills
Have the passion
Have the will
She knows how to use them
She is resourceful

The spark

Many struggle to find their spark
But she finds it by being honest with herself
Learning as much as possible
Listening to the little voice of reason in her head
And following her passion
She prays for guidance when she is lost
She asks for advice when she is lost
It's easy for her to find her spark
She has the spark
She finds it by being true to herself

Magic of Sleep

She believes in the magic of sleep
A quiet rest
To reset
And to re-energize
She believes in the magic of sleep

She is a giver

Giving makes her happy
She gives with all her heart
She is such a giver

Her reward

She is a business lady
She is a working lady
She is a leading lady
She is an exceptional lady
And she works exceptionally
She has the patience
She has the virtue
She has the confidence
Her reward is well-deserved
She deserves her reward

Hope

When the sun shines
Be hopeful
Find hope in the sun

Faith

When the sun shines
Be faithful
Find faith in the sun

Inspiration

When the sun shines
Be inspired
Find inspiration in the sun

Motivation

When the sun shines
Be motivated
Find motivation in the sun

Happiness

When the sun shines
Be happy
Find happiness in the sun

Joy

When the sun shines
Be joyful
Find joy in the sun

Grace

When the sun shines
Be graceful
Find grace in the sun

Laughter

When the sun shines
Lighten up and laugh a little
Find laughter in the sun

Ambition

When the sun shines
Be Ambitious
Find ambition in the sun

Drive

When the sun shines
Be driven
Find your drive in the sun

Comfort

When the sun shines
Be comfortable
Find comfort in the sun

Growth

When the sun shines
Focus on growth
Find growth in the sun

Meditate

When the sun shines
Draw energy from the sun
Find meditation in the sun

Thankful

When the sun shines
Be thankful
Find thankfulness in the sun

Be prayerful

Be prayerful
Brighter days are on the way
You will find your sunshine
And you will find your happiness

Be hopeful

Be hopeful
Brighter days are on the way
You will find what your heart desires

Find your soul

When you are lost
I pray that you find your soul
When your stomach is empty
I pray that you find your soul
When you are thirsty
I pray that you find your soul
When you face anguish and adversity
I pray that you find your soul
In your trying and desperate times
I pray that you find your soul

Secure yourself

Secure your heart from heartbreak
Give your love to all
But give special love to those who deserve it
Secure your essence from idleness
Make time for everything
But make special time for yourself, your friends
And your family
Make time for your hopes and dreams
And for your desires
Secure your soul and spirit from breaking
You have the soul and spirit of a child of God
You are strong and determined

Remember a good friend

Always remember a good friend
Appreciate them for their love
For their presence
For their time
For their presents
For their advice
And for their trust and honesty

Call a friend

In your unhappiest moments
Call a friend
Reach out to them and say, ' I need you, my friend'
I need your warmth
I need your wise words
I need your listening ears
And I need your uplifting cheers

Find your spirit

In your unhappiest moments
Find your spirit, it sets you free
It reminds you that you are strong
That your mind is free
Free to see the little light in the darkness
Free to imagine what can be

Within

Find the big fish within you
Your efforts will mirror it conquering the sea
Find the big eagle within you
Your efforts will mirror it conquering the sky
Find the big lion within you
Your efforts will mirror it conquering the land

Remember

Remember those people who help you
Those who listen to you
Those who appreciate you
Those who bring happiness to you
Those who recognize your efforts
Those who grow with you
Those who suffer with you
Those who fail with you
Those who fall with you
Remember them all, they are your people

Honest

God bless you for being honest
Honest with yourself
Honest with your feelings
And being honest with your thoughts
When you are honest, you are free
And when you are free, you are happy

Emotional healing

I welcome emotional healing
I welcome the tears
I welcome the laughs
I welcome the smiles
And I welcome the hugs

Spiritual healing

I welcome the spirit
I welcome the prayers
I welcome the meditation
I welcome the beauty of nature
I welcome forgiveness into my heart
I welcome the spiritual healing

Physical healing

I welcome the sleep
I welcome the meditation
I welcome the relaxation
I welcome the exercise
I welcome the warmth
I welcome the physical healing

Personal healing

I welcome the time dedicated to oneself
The time to heal, the time to learn
The time to rediscover self-worth and grow
I welcome the time for reflection
The time to have hopes and dreams
I welcome the personal healing

Professional healing

I welcome the chances
I welcome the challenges
I welcome the knowledge
I welcome the skills
I welcome the risks
I welcome the rewards
I welcome the professional healing

Full healing

My healing is incomplete
If I don't thank and praise God for it
In my happiest moments
When the sun is shining brightly upon me
I welcome the full healing of the mind, body and soul

Mental healing

I welcome the pure thoughts
I welcome the positive thoughts
I welcome the challenging thoughts
I welcome the happy thoughts
I welcome the healing thoughts
I welcome the spiritual thoughts
I welcome the creative thoughts
I welcome the careful thoughts
I welcome the mental healing

Rediscover happiness:
peace of mind

I deserve to be happy
To have peace of mind
To have a well-balanced life
To be well-established in life
I pray for lovely days
And quiet nights

Rediscover happiness: point of view

My point of view is clear
I pray to see the good in bad
And to see the bad in good
To have my heart in the right place
To have my mind in the right place
For God gives me clarity
That is my point of view

Rediscover happiness: the right condition

I am not perfect, I am just right
I am in the right condition
I am inspired
To do what is right
To be better
And to do better

I am not perfect, I am just right
I am in the right condition
I am inspired

Rediscover happiness: the right direction

I am on the right path
I will not derail
I will find what I am looking for

I am in the right direction

Rediscover happiness: gratitude and kindness

Exercise gratitude, it's good for the heart

Exercise kindness, it's good for the soul

Rediscover happiness:
these hands

I am grateful
For what these hands can do
I am able
These hands put food on my table
Dear God, I am thankful for these hands

Rediscover happiness: Happy relationships

I pray for happy relationships

Strong relationships

Fulfilling relationships

And empowering relationships

I pray for relationship growth for myself and others

Receive my hug

Receive my hug
God knows I need one too

I'm fond of your pleasantness
I feel compassion when I see you
In your presence
My reaction is to embrace you
My hug is a gesture
Of me pouring love into your heart
If you're in any pain
My warm hug is your painkiller
If you're hurting
You can cry on my shoulder
If your spirit is broken
My hug is there to comfort you
I appreciate you deeply
Feel the bond of our trust and honesty in this hug
Receive my hug with open arms

She is candid

Always a happy soul
Rich in thought
You wake up feeling powerful and strong
You found your voice
Always a thought provoker
Always a candid talker
You take care of business
But most importantly, you are
A family woman
A friendly woman
An excellent woman
An important woman
An empathetic, determined
Intelligent, truthful and honest woman

From the dark winters

From those dark winters
I come out stronger than ever
Focused on life and happiness
Focused on hope and faith
I am a lover of life and a beacon of happiness
Praying for joy like no other
I love being myself, unapologetic
My daily motto is, 'Praise be to God'
Thankful to God every day
As I chase my sunshine
Smiling deeply, glowing inside
And shining my light
I am all the positivity I embody
I am life, I am hope
And I am happiness

Thoughts on forgiveness

<u>Part 1</u>

Through all the things I've been through
Good and bad
I learned to forgive
I received the gift of friendship
And the gift of healing through the restoration
Through forgiveness
I found happiness
I found peace

Thoughts on forgiveness

<u>Part 2</u>

All my struggles, doubts
Fears, pain and loss
Prepared me for something better
Better physical, emotional and spiritual health
Through forgiveness
I found happiness
I found peace

Thoughts on forgiveness

<u>Part 3</u>

In those trying times
I realized the importance of friendship
Good friends, those that pray for your happiness
True friends who tell it like it is
Real friends who understood my real pain
Who listened to me and gave me hope
Through forgiveness
I found happiness
I found peace

Thoughts on forgiveness

<u>Part 4</u>

Moving on from bitterness

And welcoming forgiveness

Blessings will follow me

God will show wonders through me

Interesting thought, there is to 'give' in forgiveness

I give positivity and let love win

And through forgiveness

I found happiness

I found peace

Thoughts on forgiveness

<u>Part 6</u>

When it comes to painful and bad past experiences
I learned to fight all the powers formed against me
My heart forgiving, my mind forgetting
Finally letting go
And seeking self-restoration
Through forgiveness
I found happiness
I found peace

Big everything

Everything about her is big
Her God is big
And her prayers are big
Her love for family and friends is big
Her heart is big
As she is kind, caring and cheerful
Her mentality is big, she works hard
Her energy is big and she strives
Her thirst for excellence is big, she excels
Her patience is big, she waits for better things
Her substance is big; she is a woman of God
Her confidence is big; she is such a strong
And inspired woman

Patience, passion, peace and light

Rejoice, there are more milestones ahead
Rejoice, enjoy your life
Cheers to new growth, new success and taking bigger steps
To new dreams and pursuits
In the right direction
God leads you and clears your path
You have seen it all
Been through it all
The loss, the failure, the pain
Still, you came out stronger than ever
Honouring your years of success
Years of growth and building your family
You believe in God, you believe in yourself
You are such a confident woman
Cheers to more years of success, excellence
Patience, passion, peace and light

Believe in breakthroughs

You believe in prayer
You find strength in God
You believe in breakthroughs
You work hard to make things happen
You believe in your dreams
You believe in your plans
You trust your self-confidence
You trust your self-worth
You trust in love, humility and kindness
You give as much as you receive
Your motto is, 'God is gracious'
Wherever you go, you with grace
Prayerful as always
The blessings of God are upon you

She dwells in the blue ocean

She knows her true worth
She believes in her self-value
She understands self-growth
When others dwell in the red ocean
She dwells in the blue ocean
She is different
Being different makes her confident
And it makes her happy

She sees the sun and clouds

She is well prepared
She prepares for uncertainty
She understands risks and opportunities
She sees the sun and clouds

She makes it happen

She does not wait for it to happen
She makes it happen
She is patient and resilient, but still
She weathers the storm, she makes it happen

She seizes the moment

Before it slips away
She will gather enough courage and strength to grab it
She is patient and resilient, but still
She will seize the moment

Momentum

Before it slips away
She will gather enough courage and strength to grab it
She is patient and resilient, but still
She will thrive on the momentum

The work of her hands

She believes in the work of her hands
She finds enthusiasm through meaningful work
The work she loves inspires her
She believes in the work of her hands

She has expectations

She has expectations
She has the right attitude to reach them
Not only can she describe them
She will put her expectations into action
She believes in the work of her hands
She believes in her fruitful thoughts
She believes in her pioneering spirit

TENDAI M. SHABA

She believes in extraordinary things

Her mind is capable
Her spirit is capable
There's always room for improvement
She believes in the work of her hands
She believes she can do extraordinary things

She is always under construction

God is not done working wonders in her life
She is not perfect, she is good enough
She is always learning and trying new things
To make herself bigger and better

She is always under construction

HAPPINESS ☺

Tears of joy

Cry a little in your happiest moments
Feel the tears of joy

Strong woman

You evade the stones they throw at you
You break down the barriers they set for you
You are a strong woman
With a strong will
A strong mentality
And strong feelings
God gives you strength
You embody the strength of a woman

Independent woman

On your own two feet
You stand majestically in your shoes
Shoes only you can walk in
Your shoes fit, and your skin fits too
Your space is in order
Your numbers are in order
Your spirituality is in order
God gives you freedom
You embody the independence of a woman

Excellent woman

Your excellence is not feminine
Your excellence is simply excellence
You command every room with your brilliance
You are a woman of influence and substance
You keep learning
Growing and adapting
God gives you excellence
You embody the excellence of a woman

Brave woman

You go where they doubted you'd reach
Words of courage flow from your lips when you speak
They listen and still doubt
But you prove them wrong anyhow
You have your fears and doubts
But you still conquer
You are brave enough
God gives you courage
You embody the bravery of a woman

An organized and curious woman

On her watch, everything is in place
She might make some changes, still
Everything is in place
Looking for ways to make things better
Curious to know
How things work, how things are done
She is always learning
To be better and to do better
God gives her direction
She is an organized and curious woman

Spiritual woman

Her lips know the sweet taste of prayer
And positivity
Her energy is spiritual
She works hard and God blesses her
Her thoughts are spiritual
Always yearning
To grow her mind, body and soul
God gives her purpose and meaning
She is a spiritual woman

S h e   h a s   w i n g s

She has wings
She will fly
Her wings are so strong
Wings of steel, not wings of wax
She will fly high, she will reach the max
Because she has the patience
And she's willing to try, she has a strong will
She's willing to learn
And she's willing to fall, to fail
Just so she can fly high
She has the wings
She will fly

She becomes

She goes
Where her ambitions take her
She understands her thoughts and feelings
She outgrows
Those who do not grow with her
She becomes
What her dreams tell her

Powder

I see you covered
In that facial powder, an extension
They say the powder is an extension of your beauty
I say
You are beautiful with or without the powder
Let them see
Your inner and outer beauty
God-given beauty, of the heart and mind
Such beauty you cannot find in the powder

Inspired woman

From a little girl with big dreams
To a young lady breaking barriers
To an inspired woman in the driving seat
No longer a mere passenger along the ride
To a woman in the spotlight
No longer a shadow in the background
A truly inspired woman

A woman with a plan

She's gratitude
She's growth
She's grace
Her motto is, 'I can do all things'
In God, family and friends, I find strength
She wakes up every morning and says
I am excellence
I am determination
I have my struggles, my challenges
But, I move with a plan
Not just any plan, but God's plan
Because of God, I have a future
I am a woman with a plan

Her eyes

See the world through her eyes and she will open yours
You will see more
Where others see competition
She sees the opportunity for harmony and self-growth
See the world through her eyes and she will open yours

Her lips

Her lips know only the truth
And constructive talk
Her lips know the taste of prayer
And uplifting talk
Her lips know the essence of wisdom
A talk with her is an insightful talk

Her mind

Her mind is golden
You can find gold when you explore her mind
Her mind is at peace
She has mastered her priorities
She has mastered her time
Her choices are golden
Her timing is golden
And her decisions are golden
She is a golden woman
A woman with a golden mind

Her shoes

Her shoes fit
You can see how she walks, so majestically
You can put whatever price on her shoes
And she'll tell you she deserves to walk in them
She deserves to walk in those shoes

Elite mentality

Woman of quality, you
Woman of ability, you
Woman of substance, you
Woman of empathy, you
Woman of ambition, you
You flourish in your own space
You prosper at your own pace
Above all, you are a woman who
Puts God and family first
You are a woman of pure feelings
You are an elite woman

Cultured woman

I am
Proudly a cultured woman
A woman who has a special place
A recognized woman
A modern woman who
Represents all the strong
Traditional and
Enterprising women before me

She believes

She believes
That it is better to be compassionate
She is the true meaning of mercy
She believes
That it is better to forgive
She is the true meaning of kindness
She believes
That she is a transformed woman
A phenomenal woman
Aiming higher and higher as she goes
With a positive outlook on life
To keep growing
To do better and to be better
She believes

A woman on the rise

You are a woman on the rise
A woman of steel, so resilient
And hardworking
Your resiliency is a major key to success
You rise and lift those around you
You are inspired and you inspire others
You are a woman on the rise

They will remember you

Your smile is hard to forget
Your laugh, hard to forget
Your vibrancy, hard to forget
Your kindness and care, hard to forget
They will remember you

Extraordinary woman

No ordinary woman, you
Extraordinary you
A selfless person, a source of inspiration
You inspire others
To do better and to be better
You keep rising
And lifting those around you
Your words of wisdom are appreciated
Your guidance is appreciated
Your determination, kindness
Thoughtfulness and humility are all appreciated
You are the perfect example of excellence
The embodiment of greatness
No ordinary woman, you
Extraordinary you

You are truly one of a kind

Charisma wears your face
Ever cheerful
Hope wears your face
Ever hopeful
Intelligence wears your face
Ever bright
You are genuine, how God intended
Outstanding as you stand, strong-willed
A woman with a master plan
Outspoken, a woman who speaks her mind
With a thoughtful mind, a golden heart
And caring hands
You are truly one of a kind

Coming your way

God's purpose shall be known
And for you, my friend
You should be strong
Continue to be prayerful
And I pray your lips do not rest
Continue to be hopeful
I pray your heart continues to believe
You are a woman of faith
Determined and hardworking
Deserving everything good
That is coming your way
God be praised

A woman on the move

Your lips know the taste of wisdom
Your words are wise
Your eyes know the sight of beauty
You appreciate beautiful things
Your heart knows the power of love
Your feelings are powerful
You work hard
To find and sustain stability
To have a happy home
To push yourself and others
You are different, your perspective is unique
You are a woman on the move
A woman with a plan

S w e e t n e s s

I am sweetness and honey
I am a flower that attracts honeybees
My existence is poetic
My presence is poetic
My life story is poetic
Spoken words about me are always sweet
Sweet as honey
I am sweet because I am kind and generous
My motto is, 'Be a beacon of compassion'
To show empathy
And to be thoughtful
To work hard, just as hard
As bees work hard to make honey
To believe in my ideas, to explore the horizon
To experience all the sweet and beautiful things
To continue to pray
To remember God
And always believe in a new dawn

Counting my blessings

Not a single day will go by
Without counting my blessings
Having prayer on my lips
Love in my heart
And ambition on my mind
Not a single day will go by
Without saying grace and having faith
God blesses me
And I am thankful
God favours me
And I am grateful
Not a single day will go by

You deserve

Forever thankful, that you are
Gratitude defines you
So much love and compassion in your heart
Kindness defines you
You are determined
No matter how many times you fail
You keep trying
Determination defines you
You learn from life situations
Because they define who you are
A kind, resilient and determined person
I pray God clears your path so you find favour
You deserve
All the good things coming your way

A stone that stands out

Precious you are
You are like a stone that stands out
A stone that withstands all the pressure
Like the stone, you are strong
God gives you strength
And you find strength in God
Full of life, appreciative of the simple things
Adaptable, you go where your ambitions
And passions take you
Your thoughts are golden
Your mind is golden
And your hands are caring
God bless you for building a family
And a home
You are indeed precious

Hope dwells in your heart

You are hope
Hope dwells in your heart
God knows where you're coming from
And clears your new path
So you can be all you strive to be
So you can do all things you hope to do
You are a strong woman
With a heart filled with love and hope
A woman who has faith in God

Ripe fruit

You are a tree that bears ripe fruit
The embodiment of God's grace, you
You are a fruitful and graceful person
A well-balanced person
You live and you learn
You love and you forgive
You work hard to achieve the stability
Freedom and comfort in your life
You move mountains with faith
And hope dwells in your heart
You are a tree that bears ripe fruit
The embodiment of God's grace, you

A h e a r t s o p u r e

A heart so pure
One that appreciates the purity
Of feelings and all matters of the heart
You are a strong woman, pure in heart
Strong-willed and hardworking
Your destiny is in your hands
For God clears the path for you
To be all you can be, to do all you can do
You are inspired and fearless
You are the brightest star in the sky

A bright star in the sky

Hearts don't come bigger than yours
A heart filled with love and kindness
A heart filled with joy
With a strong heart, you are a fighter
You fight with God by your side
God makes your path clear
You are a bright star in the sky

Motherly moments

I appreciate every motherly moment
Those moments with you
Moments of such motherly experience
A taste of your motherly love
A feel of your motherly touch
And the gifts from your motherly hands
You encourage learning and growth
All thanks to your motherly care
Your motherly advice
And your motherly flow
Your flow of knowledge
Your flow of understanding
And your motherly ability to create
Motherly moments

A river that flows with grace

You are a river that flows with grace
You bring joy
You are a shining light in the dark
The embodiment of God's grace
Nothing rivals your thirst for knowledge
Your loving and caring heart
Your passion to be better
And to do better
You show kindness and care
You have a big warm heart
You are truly graceful
You are truly full of grace
You are the embodiment of God's grace

You are a blessing

More blessings to you
On your journey to find comfort and stability
You are the master of your destiny
You find the courage to move on
You find the strength to move on
Your mind is big, your heart is bigger
You have been through so much
But you are not alone, God is with you
Your family and friends are with you
They love and appreciate you
They believe in you
And you are truly a blessing in their lives
Remember that
You are a blessing

Golden

She sees the world
The way she sees it
Through her eyes, she builds her world
With hard work, dedication
And discipline
So wise, she is under the umbrella of wisdom
She takes on the world with precision
She owns her choices and decisions
She sees the world
The way she sees it
She sees that the essence of family is golden
That kindness is golden
That growth and stability are golden
She is golden

Virtue

She wakes up every morning
With a prayer on her lips
For God to bless her
And her family
She is patient
She is thankful
She is kind and generous
She believes in herself
To make things happen, whatever it takes
Such is her patience
Her virtue

A warrior

She is eager
She is mindful
She is strong
She is fruitful
She marches with intuition
She marches with intelligence
Focused and driven
She is a child of God
A firm believer, a warrior

A little laugh, a little smile

She smiles
And smiles some more
She laughs
And laughs some more
She is cheerful
Such is her cheerful soul
A traveller, she loves to explore
She is driven by optimism
She always remembers to smile
She always remembers to laugh
Her remedy for the day
A little laugh and a little smile

A fruitful garden

The embodiment of a rich garden, you
You embody a fruitful garden
Your inner beauty is rich
And your outer beauty is rich
You embody the essence of hospitality
You grow
You bear fruits
And you survive
A friend sees empathy in you
Determination
Intelligence
Thoughtfulness and
Honesty
You are the embodiment of a rich garden
A fruitful garden, you

Precious

She is precious
And understands that time is precious
That love is precious
That kindness, generosity
Humility and thoughtfulness
Are all precious
She is driven by ambition
And strength, that of a lioness
Majestic in her ways
Because God gives her strength
She is precious

Lioness

Knowing you
I have known kindness
Knowing you
I have known generosity
Being with you is an inspiration
You are kind, generous and inspirational
Your motto is, 'I am determined'
You embody courage
And you overcome
You believe in the armour of God
You go for what you want
You possess the strength
That of a lioness
I admire the woman you have become
A warm-hearted and supportive woman
An inspired woman

Eager and willing

I have known how to be eager
To go for my dreams
I have known how to be willing
To learn new things
To plan and execute
Driven by ambition
And strength, that of a lioness
My pride is my family
And my family is my pride
I am eager and willing

Diligent

She believes in herself
Values her self-confidence and her self-worth
She values knowledge and wisdom
And most importantly
She values her time
She guards her time with care
Because time has taught her
How to be willful
How to be strong
How to think
And how to be diligent

Simply amazing

More blessings to you, you have a heart full of love
More blessings to you, you lead with love
More blessings to you, you embrace your spirituality
More blessings to you, you are spirited
More blessings to you, you are simply amazing
More blessings to you, you value your family
More blessings to you, you possess the power of imagination
To create beautiful things
And to feel beautiful things
Such is your imagination
More blessings to you
You are simply amazing

You shall grow

You shall grow
Smile, just smile
God shall increase your happiness
Do just do
God shall increase your worth
Work, just work
God shall increase your wealth
Pray, just pray
God shall increase your favour
Learn, just learn
God shall increase your knowledge
Be kind, caring and generous
God shall increase your growth
To grow into the best version of yourself
Because you have faith in God
And God has faith in you
You shall grow
In God's hands, you shall grow

A c o n s t a n t r e m i n d e r

A constant reminder that you have faith
That you are faithful
And that your loved ones have faith in you
A constant reminder that you have a good heart
That you are thoughtful
And that your loved ones appreciate you
A constant reminder that you have passion
That you're driven
And that your loved ones see your determination
This is a constant reminder to you
To continue having faith in God
Continue working hard
Continue exploring, to find wonder
You are a travelling soul and a free thinker
Go where your thoughts take you
And go where your heart leads you

Star of the sea

She wakes up with a prayer on her lips
She says
The brightest star in the sky is all I dream to be
To be God-fearing, to be all I can be
I pray to be virtuous, virtuous me
I pray God opens my eyes, so I can see
To see that I'm special
To see that I can be all I desire to be
Blessed with a devoted spirit
To find the good in myself and others
To break barriers for myself and others
To expand my knowledge, so I can grow
Into the person, I'm destined to be
I am virtuous
The brightest star of the sea

Witness me

Witness me as I journey
On this path to realizing myself
On this path of greatness
As I pursue happiness
For myself and others
Witness me as I show gratitude
Thankful for all good things, I thank God
Thankful for this beautiful life
Witness me as I break barriers
Determined to win, no matter what it takes
God will reward my patience in the end
Witness me as I pray
Always remembering to be grateful
To be kind and generous
And to be determined
Witness me

Captivating

There's something about her
She is beautiful
A beautiful flower
Her beauty is captivating
Mesmerizing inner and outer beauty
She has a beautiful devoted spirit
The spirit responsible for her growth
And her happiness
A determined spirit, a prayerful soul
Above all things, her priority is God
The God who blessed her with such beauty
She has a beautiful devoted spirit
To show kindness and care
To be courageous, to work hard
To educate herself and prosper
There's something about her
She is beautiful
Her beauty is captivating

Gracious

I am confident
Because God blessed me with confidence
I am a gentle river
Because God blessed me with calmness
I flow with God
I flow with composure
I flow with inspiration
I flow with aspiration
To achieve all things
In the name of God
My motto is, 'I think it. I can do it'
Because I believe in God
And my God is gracious

Victorious

Something about her
She is willful
She is powerful
She is victorious
She moves at her own pace
Aligned with God's plan for her
Because she believes in God
She is destined to go places
She has a creative spirit
And a creative voice
Her motto is, 'I am confident. I am spiritual.'
She is willful
She is powerful
And she is victorious

Going with grace

Wherever you go, you go with grace
You, the embodiment of God's grace
On your path of excellence, you go with grace
With determination
Every challenge you embrace
With commitment
You gracefully run your race
With leadership and compassion
You make friends who become your family
Friends who acknowledge your passion
Friends who recognize your selflessness
Friends who admire your dedication
And friends who appreciate your humility
Wherever you go, you go with grace

A happy soul

So in touch, you are
With your thoughts and feelings
With your inner and outer beauty
You continue to smile
Even in your trying times
You find happiness in the simple things
The little things
And the good things you are blessed to have
So in touch, you are
With your thoughts and feelings
A happy soul

Fulfilment

Good things happen to you
Nice things happen to you
Amazing things happen to you
Remarkable things happen to you
You work hard
And you pray harder
To your heart's content

Happy seat

You are happy where you sit
You deserve that seat
You work hard
You pray harder
To your heart's content

Happy thoughts

You reflect on your happy moments
Your energy feeds on
That remarkable feeling of happiness
That feeling of overwhelming joy
Despite what you are going through
You always focus on your happy thoughts

Lady of delight

You are a delightful lady
The embodiment of joy
You work hard and God rewards you
With the desires of your heart

Joyful every day

Above all, you focus on the joy
You find joyful moments
A life full of joy
A calm and comfortable life
Filled with love and kindness
And hope for a brighter tomorrow
You are joyful every day

Confident every day

Above all, you focus on confidence
Believing in yourself
Believing in your decisions
Believing in your choices
You are a confident woman
A woman with a plan
You are confident every day

Calm and collected every day

Above all, you focus on calmness
No decision is rushed
No choice is rushed
You take your time
You believe that good things take time
You are calm and collected

Calm and collected every day

Above all, you focus on calmness
No decision is rushed

Patient woman

Above all, you focus on your patience
No matter how long you wait
Your eyes remain on the prize
You hold on to your dreams
You push on, patiently
You take your time
You believe that good things take time
You are a patient woman

Satisfaction

The desires of your heart
To your heart's content
All yours, because you give it your all
God bless the work of your hands
You work hard
And you pray harder
For the desires of your heart
To your heart's content

A happy attitude

A lady with a great attitude
The attitude of a beloved Queen
The attitude of a lioness
You face your great challenges
With a great attitude
A powerful attitude
Above all, your thoughts are happy
You are a lady with a happy attitude

Happy with yourself

You are happier when you are yourself
In tune with your gracious soul
You bring warmth and kindness to the world
Your smile is hard to fake
Your laugh is hard to fake
You are happy with who you are becoming
Happy with the work of your hands
You are happy with yourself

The simple things

She is here for the simple things
She appreciates them, she is down-to-earth
A cup of her favourite beverage
A plate of her favourite meal
A deep conversation with a loved one
Taking a walk in the park
Experiencing nature and its natural beauty
She is here for the simple things
She appreciates them, she is down-to-earth

The little things

She is here for the little things
She appreciates them, she deserves them
The random acts of kindness
The politeness
And the gratefulness
These little things go a long way
She is here for the little things
She appreciates them, she deserves them

The good things

She works hard
To have the good things she has
She works hard to have balance in her life
Her priorities are straight
She knows exactly what she wants
She demands excellence in her pursuits
She works hard
To have the good things she has

The important things

Her priorities are straight
She knows the important things in her life
Her spiritual life
Her work-life balance
Her family and friends
Her interests and ventures
And her plans and ambitions
Her priorities are straight
She knows the important things in her life

Good words

I welcome the good words
They are good for me

Kind words

I welcome the kind words
They are good for me

T E N D A I   M .   S H A B A

Honest words

I welcome the honest words
They are good for me

Wise words

I welcome the wise words
They are good for me

Lovely words

I welcome the lovely words
They are good for me

Lovely words

I welcome the lovely words
They are good for me

U p l i f t i n g   w o r d s

I welcome the uplifting words
They are good for me

Volumes

She is not boastful
She is not loud
She is not arrogant
And she is not ignorant
Her humility speaks volumes
Her happiness speaks volumes
And her wisdom speaks volumes

On-time

She tries her best to be on-time
She respects her time and your time
She is happy when you respect time too
Because time is precious

Listener

She listens before she speaks
And when she speaks, she is confident
Confident in the way she speaks
Confident in the way she thinks
She listens before she speaks
She is a good listener

Pleasantness

She is simply pleasant
Her words are wise
Her smile is beautiful
Her laughter is captivating
And her pleasantness is precious

Understanding

She is happy
That she's an understanding person
And asks God for guidance
She believes in God
That is the source of her true happiness

The wells of happiness

She draws from the wells of happiness
Every day
She yearns for the overwhelming joy
She knows what makes her happy
And focuses on her happiness
Every day
She draws from the wells of happiness

The cup of happiness

She drinks from the cup of happiness
Every day
She yearns for the overwhelming joy
She knows what makes her happy
And focuses on her happiness
Every day
She drinks from the cup of happiness

Being happy

She has fears
She has her doubts
She can cry, be anxious and self-destruct
But
She would rather focus on being happy

She wears it

Happiness
She wears it like a yellow dress

She wears it

Happiness
She wears it like a yellow dress

Doing well and being good

She focuses on doing well

And being good

That is what makes her happy

Fighter

Through the hardships
The setbacks
The frustrations and disappointments
She continues to fight
She is happy with her fighting spirit
She is a strong woman
She is a fighter

Medicine

A happy heart is good medicine; it heals your broken spirit
A kind and generous heart is good medicine
Happy thoughts are good medicine
A joyful heart is good medicine, it lifts you up
Be joyful
Be happy
That is good medicine

I am a strong woman, still

When she said
Being a strong woman can be tiring
I felt that, I'm sending you hugs
She then said hugs aren't enough
I need to be under an umbrella of hope
To ensure the security of my thoughts
And feelings
I need a shield against self-doubt
I need my peace and sanity
I need my comfort and stability
In those moments when fear creeps in
When I become anxious
And cry myself to sleep
The source of my strength is deep
But sometimes I feel weak
Being a strong woman can be tiring
But I keep going, I keep moving
My strength is real
Because God gives me strength
I am a strong woman, still

Be warm: thankfulness

Be warm
Show thankfulness

Be warm: thankfulness

Be warm
Show thankfulness

Be warm: kindness

Be warm
Show kindness

Be warm: kindness

Be warm
Show kindness

Be warm: thoughtfulness

Be warm
Show thoughtfulness

Be warm: generosity

Be warm
Show generosity

Be warm: generosity

Be warm
Show generosity

Be warm: humility

Be warm
Show humility

Be warm: love and affection

Be warm

Show love and affection

Be warm: understanding

Be warm
Show understanding

Be warm: gratefulness

Be warm
Show gratefulness

Be warm: warmth

Be warm
Show warmth

Pure in heart

For those
Lucky enough to experience her love
Lucky enough to experience her kindness
They know she is pure in heart
Her God is real
Her smile is real
Her touch is real
Her talk is real
Her glow is real
Her essence is real
Her substance is real
Her virtue is real
Her strength is real
Her warmth is real
Her faith is real
Her hope is real
And her love is real
She is pure in heart

Discipline

She has wounds
She has scars
She has failed
She has fallen
She has her struggles
She has troubles
Despite all that
She maintains her focus
She maintains her drive
She maintains her confidence
And when she conquers all
Through the strength God gives her
She rejoices
She is such a happy woman
And a disciplined woman

About the author ♠

Tendai M. Shaba is a Malawian writer, poet, activist and author of moments to cherish (2020) and a lady in a yellow dress (2023). He has officially been involved as an activist in numerous campaigns on mental health awareness, women empowerment, labour productivity and climate change. You can access more of his work here: http://www.tendaishaba.com/

Acknowledgements ♥

The colour yellow is often associated with sunshine and happiness. These poems are written to inspire good emotional health for all who seek sunshine and happiness within themselves. As much as we are inspired by the good and beautiful things around us, our focal point of inspiration is the lady in a yellow dress.

Pachulu Publishing, Malawi, 2023

www.ingramcontent.com/pod-product-compliance
Lightning Source LLC
Chambersburg PA
CBHW020337160726
47992CB00004B/1879